ESSAYS ON TYRANNY

RESISTING TRUMP'S ATTACK ON DEMOCRACY

JIM VINCENT

Jim Vincent

© 2025 Jim Vincent

All rights reserved.

No part of this publication may be reproduced, stored in a retrieval system, or transmitted in any form or by any means—electronic, mechanical, photocopy, recording, or otherwise—without the prior written permission of the publisher, except for brief quotations used in reviews, articles, or scholarly analysis.

This is a work of nonfiction. Every effort has been made to ensure accuracy. Any errors are the responsibility of the author. Opinions expressed are the author's own and do not represent any organization or institution. This book is for informational and educational purposes only and does not constitute legal advice. The author is not a lawyer and makes no guarantees regarding legal outcomes. Readers should consult qualified legal counsel or trusted advocacy organizations before taking action based on this material.

Cover design by Jim Vincent.

Published by Vincent Press

Printed and distributed by IngramSpark

Printed in 2025 • VP Edition 1.0.is

ISBN: 978-1-7641693-6-3 (paperback)

For more information, visit: https://jimvincent.us

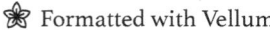 Formatted with Vellum

"America will never be destroyed from the outside. If we falter and lose our freedoms, it will be because we destroyed ourselves." — Abraham Lincoln

CONTENTS

Introduction	vii
Prologue	1
1. The Road to Tyranny – But Not Without a Fight	5
2. The Descent — How Tyranny Took Hold	9
3. The Seizure — What Trump Is Taking and How We Fight Back	14
4. How We Fight Back – The Playbook for Resistance	19
Appendix A: Timeline of Tyranny — Key Events in 2025	23
Appendix B: Orders of Control — Executive Actions Under Trump's Second Term	25
Appendix C: Lessons for Resistance — Echoes of History and Warnings for Now	27
Reader's Guide: Essays on Tyranny	29
Epilogue	33
Bibliography	35
Supplemental Sources	37
About the Author	39
Also by Jim Vincent	41

INTRODUCTION

―――― ✦ ――――

This book is not written from theory. It is written from recognition. The signs of tyranny are no longer distant signals or historical parallels—they are headlines, court rulings, executive orders, and silences. We are not forecasting collapse; we are documenting its method.

Essays on Tyranny was written in the shadow of Trump's second term, but it is not about Trump alone. It is about the system that allowed him to return, the enablers who shielded him from consequence, and the people who now face a choice between surrender and defiance. It is about how democracies fall—not by sudden attack, but by slow erosion—and how they survive, only when those within them choose to resist.

This is a book for those who have stopped hoping someone else will fix it. For those who see what is happening, and are ready to act. Each chapter draws on history not to relive it, but to interrupt it. Each warning is paired with a strategy. Each account of collapse is matched by a plan to hold the line.

The essays that follow do not promise hope without struggle. They offer something deeper: a map for those who refuse to be ruled by fear. The question is no longer whether authoritarianism is rising. It is whether you will rise to meet it.

PROLOGUE

The moment America changed was not the night of an election, nor the storming of a Capitol. It was not a single law passed, a speech given, or even a verdict rendered. It was the quiet moment when people, institutions, and leaders—one by one—decided they could live with this.

They could live with an autocrat in the White House, so long as their party benefited. They could live with purges of civil servants, so long as they were not the ones fired. They could live with journalists banned, opposition leaders indicted, and the courts packed with loyalists, so long as they still had their piece of the system. Compliance was never announced; it was assumed, rationalized, accepted. And with each surrender, the impossible became inevitable.

The latest Supreme Court decisions have confirmed what history already warned: the system will not save itself. In April 2025, the Court declined to reinstate core protections for free elections and again shielded Trump's efforts to control voting oversight and purge opposition candidates from ballots. Simultaneously, Trump's Department of Justice has accelerated investigations into prosecutors and judges who previously ruled against him. The machinery of retribution is not being built—it is already operating.

We have seen this before. Democracies do not fall in explosions of violence, but in quiet, procedural betrayals. The Reichstag was not burned by Hitler's men, but it was used to justify his power grab. Hungary did not wake up one morning under a dictator, but it did wake up to a judiciary rewritten to serve one. Rome did not become an empire overnight, but its Senate did vote itself into irrelevance. The lesson is always the same: tyranny advances when people believe the system will hold, even as they watch it erode beneath their feet.

The courts have given him immunity. His party has sworn its loyalty. The press that once mocked him now adjusts to his rule, fearful of losing access or becoming the next target. The laws that once protected us are now being rewritten to protect him instead. In Florida, Texas, and Ohio, April saw the passage of new laws criminalizing public protests near government offices and broadening the definition of "election interference" to include peaceful demonstrations. The tools of repression grow sharper by the week.

This is not the beginning of a slide into authoritarianism. It is the final stage, where resistance either succeeds or vanishes altogether.

This book is not a warning—it is a battle plan. The fight is not theoretical; it has already begun. What happens next will determine whether democracy survives in America or whether it joins the long list of governments that assumed they were too strong to fail.

No system will save itself. No institution will stand unless people make it stand. The question is not whether democracy is in peril. The question is what you are willing to do to stop its fall.

1

THE ROAD TO TYRANNY – BUT NOT WITHOUT A FIGHT

"The greatest danger to American freedom is a government that ignores the Constitution." - Thomas Jefferson

There is a moment in every democracy's decline when the people realize, too late, that the collapse was not sudden but gradual; that freedoms were not taken but surrendered; and that the descent was not inevitable but a choice. The story of autocracy is never a single dramatic event — it is the slow decay of institutions, the quiet resignation of those who could have stopped it, and obedience that comes before the orders are even issued. Yet, history shows us another truth: no tyrant rules alone. No regime consolidates without help. No system is beyond resistance. Every authoritarian who has seized power has faced opposition — sometimes too little, sometimes too late, but sometimes just enough. The difference between a democracy that falls and one that endures is not in the strength of the autocrat, but in the will of the people who refuse to give up.

Autocracy is never the work of a single person. Hitler did not rise without the Reichstag surrendering to him. Mussolini's power was strengthened not solely by his own force, but by institutions bending to his will. Orbán did not destroy Hungary's democracy overnight—he eroded it gradually, with the complicity of courts, media, and corporate allies. The American model is no different. Trump's rise was not an isolated achievement. He was supported by enablers in government, the press, and the business world. Judges who justified his excesses. Politicians who feared his wrath more than they valued the Constitution. Media networks that normalized his lies for profit. Corporations that financed his movement, hedging their bets on a system they thought they could control. In April 2025, we saw this strategy intensify. Major companies—including several large defense contractors and telecom firms—changed their previous positions and donated to Trump-aligned PACs after facing informal "regulatory reviews" targeting their operations. Again, power was not taken by force but gained through pressure, silence, and survival instinct. The road to tyranny is built not only by those who seize power but also by those who turn a blind eye as it happens. The history of authoritarianism teaches us that silence equals complicity, and that neutrality is an illusion. Those who think they can survive an autocracy by staying silent will find that there is no safety in submission —only a future reckoning.

Trump's first presidency was not about governance; it was about testing limits. He spent four years pushing the system, seeking weaknesses, observing which institutions resisted and which folded. When courts challenged him, he attacked their legitimacy. When the media exposed his corruption, he flooded the landscape with propaganda. When his own officials disobeyed him, he purged them. And the system adapted. Instead of rejecting him outright, it accommodated his lawlessness. Congress refused to hold him accountable. The Justice Department gradually became his personal shield. The Supreme Court, filled with loyalists, signaled its readiness to reinterpret the Constitution in his favor. The lesson was clear: the safeguards were weaker than they appeared. New revelations this spring from whistleblowers inside the Department of Homeland Security show that during his first term, Trump's administration even kept secret internal "compliance" lists—tracking officials by loyalty metrics, with red-flag markers on those deemed disloyal to the MAGA cause. Although exposed, no one has been held accountable for their use. Instead, Trump's allies now publicly propose reviving and expanding these blacklists in a second term. Now, emboldened and unchecked, he is no longer testing. He is executing. He no longer merely suggests jailing his enemies—he is already doing it. He no longer merely courts armed militias—he pardons and protects them. He no longer hints at a one-party state—he is laying its legal groundwork. The autocracy he once toyed with is now his blueprint.

The difference between a country that becomes a dictatorship and one that resists lies not in the autocrat but in the people. Compliance makes tyranny inevitable, while resistance makes it impossible. This book will outline the path Trump has already taken, where he currently stands, and how he plans to finalize his move toward authoritarian rule.

. . .

CHAPTER 2 WILL REVEAL the damage already inflicted—how he has dismantled oversight, undermined truth, and legitimized political violence.

Chapter 3 will expose what he is seizing right now, from control over elections and law enforcement to the economy itself.

Chapter 4 will present the strategy—the tactics, actions, and movements that can stop this autocratic effort before it becomes permanent.

AUTOCRACY IS NOT JUST one event; it is a process. The past eight years have shown us that democracy is not only under threat; it has already been weakened. The institutions meant to protect it have either failed or been dismantled.

To resist effectively, we must first recognize what has already been lost. The autocracy is not coming; it is here. And it did not arrive suddenly, but gradually, as each institution bowed, each law was rewritten, and each norm collapsed.

That is where we start.

2

THE DESCENT — HOW TYRANNY TOOK HOLD

"Power is not a means; it is an end." — George Orwell

Trump is not just corrupt; he is systematically dismantling democracy. He has taken control of oversight mechanisms, gutted watchdog agencies, purged disloyal officials, and manipulated the courts to serve his interests. He has legitimized political violence, pardoning his allies and encouraging paramilitary groups to operate openly. He has criminalized opposition by using the legal system to harass, prosecute, and silence critics. He has flooded the public discourse with relentless propaganda, rendering truth irrelevant and ensuring his followers trust only him. Furthermore, he has laid the groundwork for lasting minority rule by empowering states to suppress votes, remove election officials, and overturn future results. Each of these actions follows the authoritarian playbook, yet none are completely secured. There is still time to reverse them. The first step toward autocracy is always the destruction of truth. Without truth, accountability and a shared reality vanish, making it impossible to challenge power. Trump has spent years conditioning his base to believe only him, dismissing facts that contradict his narrative as "fake news." He has normalized conspiracy theories, from election fraud lies to QAnon fantasies, until his followers accept falsehoods as fact and see reality as deception.

The Republican Party has followed suit, embracing propaganda networks that act as de facto state media. Trump's control is so absolute that his newly appointed FBI director has published a list of political enemies targeted for prosecution. The real risk isn't just that Trump lies—it's that his base wants to be deceived. They prefer his version of reality, where he is the legitimate leader, his enemies are criminals, and democracy is a sham. A nation that can't tell truth from propaganda is vulnerable to tyranny. The fight against Trump is not just political—it's a battle to restore reality itself. When lies fail to persuade on their own, autocrats turn to force. Trump has spent years encouraging violence, first through rhetoric, then through action. The January 6 insurrection wasn't just a riot—it was a test. When Republican lawmakers refused to hold him accountable, and when his supporters were praised as patriots instead of criminals, he saw the way forward. He has since pardoned convicted insurrectionists, supported white nationalist militias, and vowed to use state force against his enemies in his second term.

Republican-led states are normalizing paramilitary policing, allowing far-right groups to operate under the guise of election security and border enforcement. The message is clear: opposition will not just be discouraged—it will be dangerous. Fascism does not rise when a strongman makes threats. It rises when people believe those threats and choose silence over resistance.

Political violence is most effective when the state can make opposition itself a crime. Trump has already laid the groundwork. In his first term, he tried and failed to use the Justice Department to prosecute his rivals. Now, he is openly vowing to succeed. His newly appointed FBI director has published a list of those targeted for prosecution, and the Republican-controlled Congress is harassing and investigating prosecutors handling his cases, turning the legal system into a tool of political warfare.

The purge will escalate. The DOJ will indict, and the FBI will arrest, while state legislatures pass laws making dissent itself a criminal act. The White House has already banned AP reporters and handpicked White House correspondents for loyalty. Republican-led states have passed "anti-riot" laws that selectively criminalize left-wing protests while encouraging right-wing intimidation. But direct prosecution isn't even necessary.

Eric Adams in New York was neutralized with the mere promise of dismissing his corruption case. The media—Washington Post, Facebook, ABC, NBC, CBS, CNN—have all been brought to heel not through arrests, but through the threat of being made a target. Once autocrats begin weaponizing the legal system, conviction is optional. Compliance is enough.

Trump and his allies have dismantled oversight at every level to make these tactics unchallengeable. Watchdogs have been purged. Inspectors General have been fired. Congress, under Republican control, has abandoned its duty to hold the executive branch accountable. The Supreme Court, stacked with conservative loyalists, has consistently ruled in favor of partisan power grabs.

When precedent stood in the way, they reinterpreted the Constitution to fit Trump's needs, most notably in their July 1, 2023, ruling that granted Trump broad presidential immunity. That decision was not just about shielding him from prosecution—it was a signal. In their ruling, the presidency is now beyond the reach of the law.

The federal judiciary has been packed with Federalist Society appointees who will rubber-stamp Trump's agenda. Republican-led states have rewritten election laws to strip power from independent officials and transfer it to partisan legislatures. The system has not failed—it has been dismantled. And with every check on power removed, the final step becomes inevitable: democracy itself ceases to function.

All of this leads to the last, irreversible step—creating a one-party state. Republicans have spent decades laying the foundation, using gerrymandering, voter suppression, and legal manipulation to ensure minority rule. When the Supreme Court gutted the Voting Rights Act in 2013, Republican states moved instantly to purge voter rolls and impose restrictions that disproportionately affected Democratic voters. That was only the beginning. Now, they are going further.

In key swing states, Republican legislatures have passed laws allowing them to overturn election results. Trump has taken control of the Federal Election Commission, meaning the very rules governing elections are now under his direct authority. If results do not favor him, they will be changed. If election officials refuse to comply, they will be prosecuted. If voters still push through these barriers, gerrymandering ensures their votes won't matter. With state legislatures controlling electoral outcomes and courts backing their authority, elections will go on—but only as a formality. America will still have voting, but voting will no longer matter.

This is the moment when resistance still matters. Truth can still be defended. Political violence can still be exposed and stopped. The justice system, though compromised, has not yet been fully weaponized. State election laws, even those rewritten to favor Republicans, can still be challenged and overturned. The illusion of democracy remains—but illusions can be broken.

Authoritarianism relies not just on power, but on belief. It requires people to accept that once a system is in place, it cannot be broken. But every system of power is built by people, and what is built can be dismantled.

If Trump and his allies succeed, there will still be elections, but they will not matter. There will still be courts, but they will not deliver justice. There will still be institutions, but they will serve only the regime. That moment is not yet here—but it is closer than ever. What happens now will decide whether America remains a democracy or becomes a nation where elections are theater, opposition is criminalized, and power is permanently held by those who can manipulate the system in their favor.

The time for warnings is over. The time for action has arrived.

3

THE SEIZURE — WHAT TRUMP IS TAKING AND HOW WE FIGHT BACK

---◆---

"The march of tyranny is only halted by the resistance of those who refuse to submit." — Frederick Douglass

Trump has never been satisfied with just power. It must be total. What he already believes he has taken—the courts and justice system, oversight mechanisms, normalization of violence—is only the start. Now, he moves to complete the job. Every remaining check on his rule is being attacked. For him to finish what he started: elections must come under his direct control. Law enforcement must serve him, not the law. Dissent must be criminalized, opposition leaders silenced, and the military must be forced to obey him. The economy—employment, funding, contracts, entire industries—must become a tool for rewards and punishments.

This is not just about controlling the government but controlling the entire structure of American power.

And yet, none of this is inevitable—unless we accept it.

Trump and his allies have rewritten state election laws, stripping power from nonpartisan officials and giving it to political loyalists. Local election offices are being cleaned of career professionals and replaced with operatives who will enforce voter restrictions and, if needed, override results.

April 2025 marked a significant escalation: Georgia's legislature passed a law allowing the State Election Board—appointed by the governor—to directly take control of any county election office without judicial review. Arizona's legislature authorized removal of vote tabulation machines under vague "security concerns," even during an election. The strategy is clear: suppress votes where possible, overturn them where necessary. The legal framework for electoral theft is already in place. In key states, Trump-aligned secretaries of state now have unilateral authority to certify—or refuse to certify—results. The Federal Election Commission, increasingly partisan, is rewriting rule interpretations to favor Trump's operations.

No election is decided before the first ballot is cast—unless we accept it.

Trump's effort to take control of law enforcement is speeding up. In his first term, he demanded personal loyalty from the FBI and the Department of Justice and was often blocked. Now, he is removing those who oppose him and replacing them with supporters. His new attorney general has already indicated a willingness to prosecute political opponents, and the Republican Congress is preparing for mass arrests on claims of "election fraud" and "deep state corruption."

In April 2025, the DOJ announced "enhanced integrity reviews" of judges, prosecutors, and law enforcement officials involved in cases against Trump or his allies. This intimidating move, hidden behind bureaucratic language, effectively puts the justice system under constant political oversight.

The FBI has formalized its target list into a new "Priority Enforcement Initiative" mainly focused on political opponents and dissenters labeled as "subversive threats." Language once used for organized crime is now used against protest organizers, voting rights advocates, and investigative journalists.

If this succeeds, the Department of Justice will stop being a check on power — it will become his weapon. The FBI will no longer protect the law; it will enforce his will.

No law bends to one man's will—unless we accept it.

Beyond the Department of Justice, Trump is working to bring the military under his control. He has already begun purging high-ranking officers, forcing resignations and retirements to clear the way for loyalists who will not question his orders. His advisors have openly stated their intention to use the military domestically—as Trump already has—to crush protests, enforce political decrees, and "restore order" against his enemies.

April brought new evidence of this push. Several Pentagon watchdog offices reported unprecedented pressure from White House liaisons to produce loyalty oaths, mandatory MAGA-aligned briefings, and "political reliability assessments" for senior officers. Although quietly resisted by some in the military leadership, these demands are steadily reshaping the officer corps.

The calls to jail political opponents are not just rally rhetoric—they are policy. Trump-aligned state legislatures are drafting bills to criminalize "disloyalty to constitutional governance"—a term left intentionally vague to allow mass arrests of political opponents. Meanwhile, new media restrictions proposed for federal contracts would condition eligibility for press access on "demonstrated impartiality," a thinly veiled loyalty test.

The last step—where speaking against Trump becomes a direct path to prosecution or exile—has not yet been fully taken.

But its scaffolding is nearly complete.

No voice is silenced forever—unless we accept it.

The last unchecked frontier is the economy itself. Trump is already using mass firings, federal contracts, tax policies, and funding decisions as tools—penalizing blue states while rewarding loyalists. The goal is clear: create an economic system where businesses, industries, and entire regions must comply or face financial ruin. New developments in April 2025 show how quickly this system is changing. The Department of Commerce, now directly controlled by the White House, announced new "national security" reviews of major companies that have donated to Democratic candidates. Federal grant eligibility is now tied to "alignment with national values"—a euphemism for MAGA loyalty. Trump's campaign surrogates have issued explicit threats to Fortune 500 companies: get in line, or face "regulatory scrutiny" and "contract reassessment." Some industries—especially healthcare, education, and renewable energy—are already seeing funding cuts and expanded audits for perceived political opposition. State-level Republicans are also following suit, cutting budgets for cities, universities, and NGOs associated with Democratic causes. Florida's April budget punished four universities for hosting "unapproved speech events," reducing their state funding by 40%. The country's economic structure is being reshaped—not by market competition or democratic policy—but by authoritarian command. No economy belongs to a ruler—unless we accept it.

Trump has demonstrated his intent. His plans are no longer just ideas; the infrastructure for autocracy is being constructed in real time. Election outcomes will be manipulated. Law enforcement will serve as a political tool. Protest will be banned. The economy will be shaped to benefit the loyal and punish the opposition. And yet, none of this is certain. The path toward dictatorship only succeeds when people accept its inevitability. Every system of power is created by people, and what is created can be dismantled.

4

HOW WE FIGHT BACK – THE PLAYBOOK FOR RESISTANCE

──── ✦ ────

"The most effective way to destroy people is to deny and obliterate their own understanding of their history." — George Orwell

The battle for democracy is ongoing—neither lost nor won. Trump has employed the authoritarian playbook to dismantle the institutions that once kept power in check, yet his control remains incomplete. He has gained ground where resistance was weak but has not succeeded where it was strong. The question now is not whether he will fully take over but whether those opposing him will fight with the same relentless resolve. The warning signs are clear, as is the path forward. Scholars and historians—from Timothy Snyder's *On Tyranny* to Jason Stanley's *How Fascism Works* and Gene Sharp's studies of civil resistance—have outlined both the dangers and the strategies to oppose them. These lessons are not just historical;

they serve as instructions for action. The era of passive observation is over. The time to act is now.

Trump has depended on individuals breaking their professional codes to serve him. Lawyers, doctors, law enforcement officers, elected officials, and military personnel—each time someone chooses loyalty to him over integrity, democracy suffers. Whistleblowers must be protected. Resistors must be supported. Betrayers must be isolated. The events of April 2025 demonstrate once again that when institutions are left to defend themselves, they fall apart. Several Inspector General offices—purged without widespread protest—stand as monuments to silent compliance. To resist effectively, we must replace silence with visible, public support for those who stand firm, and visible consequences for those who betray their oaths. Authoritarianism does not appear fully formed; it is constructed gradually by those who choose to look away or go along. Trump's movement floods the world with his name, his image, his narrative. The way to counter it is not only to reject his iconography but to replace it. Make truth louder than lies. Make resistance more visible than submission.

Trump has openly declared his goal: to manipulate the electoral system so Republicans never lose again. His party has stacked courts, carried out voter purges, rewritten election laws, and is now openly overriding local election authorities. But his control is not yet complete. The only way to prevent a one-party state is to break its hold before it becomes irreversible. Challenge every restriction. Contest every purge. Defend every voter. Lawsuits against voter suppression must be filed early and everywhere. Registration efforts must be ongoing, even in places Trump considers already "won." Legal observers must be trained and deployed to monitor elections, challenge illegal interventions, and document abuses for immediate action. Neutrality is no longer a virtue; it is surrender. Every official who defends democracy must be protected, elected, or re-elected. Every official who betrays it must be exposed, opposed, and removed.

The Proud Boys, Oath Keepers, and other extremist groups are no longer fringe elements. They have been pardoned, emboldened, and now prepare for future violence openly, some under the guise of "election security." Treat them as what they are—domestic terrorists. Investigate them, prosecute them, expose their funding sources, their recruitment methods, and their networks of enablers inside police departments, sheriffs' offices, and local governments. The Pentagon, though partially purged, still holds officers loyal to constitutional governance. They must be supported. Civilian leadership must not assume loyalty—it must demand it. Transparency about military politicization efforts must become a public priority, not a secret whispered among insiders. Resistance does not mean waiting for orders. It means active disruption of every attempt to normalize authoritarian control—whether by confrontation, exposure, or simple refusal to comply. Authoritarianism thrives on fear and fragmentation. Resistance must thrive on courage and connection.

April 2025 exposed another battlefield: control of information. States are now moving to require social media platforms to certify political neutrality—a thin cover for purging dissent. Resistance must move to secure communications. Activists, journalists, and ordinary citizens alike must encrypt messages, anonymize sensitive data, and protect networks from surveillance and disruption. Alternative information channels must be built—locally, digitally, and redundantly—so that when mainstream platforms buckle, the flow of truth continues uninterrupted. Digital resistance is no longer optional. It is survival.

No one person can do everything. But everyone can do something. Some will fight with their voices, exposing lies, challenging propaganda, refusing to be silenced. Some will fight with their votes, registering, mobilizing, protecting elections at every level. Some will fight with their time, organizing communities, securing communication lines, defending the institutions that remain. Some will fight with their wallets, funding independent journalism, civil rights groups, legal challenges, and grassroots organizers. Resistance is not a single act—it is a million choices made every day. It is found in showing up to protest. In refusing to echo lies. In protecting the vulnerable. In refusing to be cowed into silence or cynicism. This is the moment when resistance must not flicker, but blaze.

History does not remember those who rationalized surrender. It remembers those who refused it. Trumpism will not end with Trump. Authoritarianism will not vanish with one defeat. But neither will democracy vanish if those who believe in it refuse to let it die. The fight is not theoretical. It is practical, immediate, and local. It is fought on school boards, in courtrooms, in statehouses, and in every place where power either bends to justice or breaks it.

Speak. Organize. Challenge. Protect. Fight. Not because victory is guaranteed, but because surrender is unacceptable. True patriotism is not obedience. It is resistance.

APPENDIX A: TIMELINE OF TYRANNY — KEY EVENTS IN 2025

———✦———

This chronology captures the most critical developments in Trump's second term to date. Each is either a legal escalation, institutional collapse, or authoritarian maneuver described in the preceding chapters. The timeline is not comprehensive—but it is sufficient to trace the pattern of power's consolidation and the erosion of democratic restraint.

- **January 20:** Trump inaugurated for a second term; outlines "America Restored" agenda.
- **February:** DOJ announces "integrity audits" of prosecutors tied to prior Trump indictments.
- **March:** FEC rewrites campaign finance enforcement protocols to eliminate bipartisan oversight.

- **April:**
    - Georgia legislature grants itself power to seize local election boards without court review.
    - Arizona authorizes mid-election removal of ballot machines under vague "security" grounds.
    - DOJ launches "Priority Enforcement Initiative" targeting dissenters as "subversive threats."
    - Department of Commerce initiates retaliatory investigations of Democratic-aligned firms.
    - Florida legislature slashes funding to four universities for "unapproved speech events."
- **May:** Federal agencies revise contract eligibility to require "alignment with national values"—a euphemism for political loyalty.
- **June:** Ohio and Texas pass laws redefining "election interference" to include peaceful protest near government offices.

History will not remember the dates alone. It will remember what the people did next.

APPENDIX B: ORDERS OF CONTROL — EXECUTIVE ACTIONS UNDER TRUMP'S SECOND TERM

--- ✦ ---

The blueprint for autocracy is being implemented through executive action, rule reinterpretation, and bureaucratic mandate. These orders represent key steps taken to consolidate control over the federal government, silence opposition, and reshape public life to serve a permanent authoritarian regime.

- **EO-2025-001:** Reinstates **Schedule F**, authorizing dismissal of civil servants deemed ideologically "unreliable."
- **EO-2025-012:** Establishes DOJ "Anti-Constitutional Actor" task force to surveil and investigate civil society critics.
- **EO-2025-023:** Authorizes state National Guards to

conduct "election integrity" operations—including monitoring ballot locations.
- **EO-2025-041:** Conditions all federal grants and contracts on receipt of an "American Values Certification," effectively blacklisting dissent.
- **Presidential Directive 17:** Directs Pentagon to conduct political loyalty audits of senior command staff.

EACH OF THESE actions is reversible—if we act in time. But left unchallenged, they will become precedent. And precedent, once normalized, becomes the next administration's foundation.

APPENDIX C: LESSONS FOR RESISTANCE — ECHOES OF HISTORY AND WARNINGS FOR NOW

———✦———

Drawn from the work of historians, dissidents, and truth-tellers—and sharpened through the pages of this book—these lessons are not abstractions. They are principles of survival. They are the guardrails that remain.

> "No system collapses in a single moment. It collapses one excuse at a time."

> "When the truth becomes optional, democracy becomes impossible."

> "Every authoritarian advance was once a tolerated exception."

"Silence is not neutral. It is how tyrants hear consent."

"The vote still counts—until you believe it doesn't."

"Power rewrites law when people stop defending it."

"History remembers the resistors—not the rationalizers."

"You do not wait to lose freedom before you defend it."

Resistance does not begin when it is safe. It begins when it is necessary. These words are not for later. They are for now.

READER'S GUIDE: ESSAYS ON TYRANNY

The Stakes

DEMOCRACY IS NOT LOST through invasion—it is surrendered through silence. *Essays on Tyranny* shows how lawlessness became law, and how every delay in resisting Trump's second-term authoritarianism moves the country closer to irreversible collapse.

The Structure

THE BOOK IS DIVIDED into four chapters: (1) the historical warning, (2) the process of authoritarian takeover, (3) the seizure of institutions, and (4) the strategy for resistance. It concludes with an epilogue and three appendices providing real-world context, legal references, and resistance lessons.

The Collapse

Trump is not an aberration. He is a culmination. From election subversion to DOJ weaponization, he has reshaped American governance to serve permanent minority rule. Each chapter shows a different layer of that transformation.

The Remedy

Resistance requires action at every level: protest, policy, legal challenge, and moral refusal. The book outlines how to protect election systems, defend dissent, expose violence, and rebuild shared truth. Resistance is not abstract. It is urgent.

What Comes Next

The future depends not on whether Trump is stopped—but on whether Americans stop believing someone else will do it for them. This is a call to civic courage and a guide to immediate action.

· · ·

Three Things to Remember

- No system saves itself.
- Tyranny thrives on delay.
- You do not wait to lose freedom before you defend it.

Action List

- Document every abuse.
- Challenge laws that criminalize dissent.
- Protect local election officials.
- Support whistleblowers and journalists.
- Fund independent watchdogs.
- Refuse propaganda; share verified truth.
- Expose enablers—economic, legal, and political.

Strategic Rationale

The authoritarian playbook depends on fear, normalization, and fragmentation. Trump's strategy is not subtle—it is cumulative. Each unchecked abuse becomes the basis for the next. To stop the collapse, we must disrupt the logic of submission. That means coordinated action, principled defiance, and unrelenting visibility.

. . .

What You Can Do

You don't have to do everything—but you must do something. Start where you are. Speak the truth in conversations that go silent. Correct the lie that elections no longer matter. Volunteer for those still fighting to protect the vote. Donate if you can, march if you're able, and organize with those who refuse to be cowed. Support independent media and civil rights groups. Stand behind whistleblowers and beside targeted communities. If you work in law, medicine, education, journalism, or public service—uphold your code and resist those who break theirs. Refuse to comply with injustice disguised as law. Make resistance visible, make courage contagious, and never let despair do the tyrant's work for him. Freedom is not defended later. It is defended now—by you.

EPILOGUE

———✦———

Democracy is never secured, only defended. It is not a fortress standing against time, but a tide held back by those who refuse to let it recede. The struggle does not end with one election, one movement, or one victory—it is a battle that must be fought, again and again, by those who will not surrender.

The great empires of history did not fall from invasion alone, but from within. They collapsed when their people accepted corruption as normal, when they looked away from abuses of power, when they convinced themselves that someone else would step up, that there was still time, that the threat was not as serious as it seemed. America is no different. The difference between a democracy that survives and one that is lost is not found in the strength of the autocrat, but in the will of the people who refuse to yield.

Some will say it is already too late. That Trump and his movement have taken too much, corrupted too many, and placed themselves beyond the reach of accountability. That no system can withstand such an onslaught. But history does not belong to those who predict failure—it belongs to those who refuse to accept it. Dictatorships fall. Tyrants are overthrown. Regimes that once seemed unshakable have collapsed overnight, not because they lost their power, but because the people they ruled lost their fear.

This fight will not be won in a single moment, but in the choices made every day. In the conversations where lies are challenged. In the protests where silence is broken. In the votes cast, the officials held accountable, the resistance that does not fade when the headlines do. Trumpism will not end with Trump. Authoritarianism will not vanish with one defeat. But neither will democracy vanish if those who believe in it refuse to let it die.

The road ahead is uncertain, but one truth remains: the time for waiting is over. The time for hoping that institutions will hold is gone. The time for action is now.

If democracy is to endure, let it endure because we fought for it. If freedom is to survive, let it survive because we refused to surrender it. If history is to remember this moment, let it remember that we did not stand aside—we stood up.

BIBLIOGRAPHY

The fight against authoritarianism is not new, nor is the playbook that Trump and his allies are following. These books provide essential historical context, strategies for resistance, and insights into the mechanisms of democratic erosion.

Snyder, Timothy. *On Tyranny: Twenty Lessons from the Twentieth Century.* Tim Duggan Books, 2017. A concise and powerful guide to resisting authoritarianism, drawing lessons from the rise of fascism and communism in the 20th century.

Stanley, Jason. *How Fascism Works: The Politics of Us and Them.* Random House, 2018. Explains how fascist movements gain power by distorting truth, creating enemies, and undermining democratic institutions.

Sharp, Gene. *From Dictatorship to Democracy: A Conceptual Framework for Liberation.* The Albert Einstein Institution, 1993. A foundational work on nonviolent resistance, detailing how civil disobedience can successfully challenge authoritarian regimes.

Orwell, George. *1984.* Secker & Warburg, 1949. A dystopian novel that serves as a prophetic warning about the dangers of propaganda, surveillance, and totalitarian control.

Arendt, Hannah. *The Origins of Totalitarianism.* Schocken Books, 1951. A seminal analysis of how totalitarian regimes arise, examining Nazi Germany and Stalinist Russia to reveal the conditions that enable autocracy.

Levitsky, Steven, and Daniel Ziblatt. *How Democracies Die.* Crown Publishing Group, 2018. A study of democratic backsliding, illustrating how elected leaders can undermine democratic norms without abolishing them outright.

Ben-Ghiat, Ruth. *Strongmen: Mussolini to the Present.* W.W. Norton & Company, 2020. Profiles autocratic leaders from Mussolini to Trump, analyzing their strategies for gaining and holding power.

Kendzior, Sarah. *Hiding in Plain Sight: The Invention of Donald Trump and the Erosion of America.* Flatiron Books, 2020. Investigates Trump's rise through the lens of oligarchy, corruption, and the long decline of American institutions.

Ricks, Thomas E. *First Principles: What America's Founders Learned from the Greeks and Romans and How That Shaped Our Country.* Harper, 2020.

Explores how the Founding Fathers studied classical philosophy and history, and how their lessons on power and corruption apply to the present.

Parker, Ashley. *The Age of Impunity: Trump, Tyranny, and the Crisis of American Democracy.* Random House, 2025. A penetrating examination of how the erosion of accountability, oversight, and democratic norms accelerated during Trump's second rise to power—and how impunity became the foundation of authoritarian rule.

These works are not just history—they are blueprints for understanding, resisting, and overcoming authoritarianism in any era.

SUPPLEMENTAL SOURCES

In addition to the historical and political works above, several major investigative reports provide critical real-time insights into the unfolding erosion of democratic governance during 2025. These reports document current developments with the same seriousness required to understand—and confront—the present crisis.

ProPublica. "Inside Trump's War on the Deep State." April 2025. A detailed investigation into how Trump's administration restructured oversight agencies, weaponized investigations, and purged perceived disloyalty across government.

Just Security. "Mapping Trump's Legal Battles and Immunity Claims." Updated April 2025. A comprehensive tracking of Trump's ongoing legal cases, immunity defenses, and efforts to expand presidential power beyond constitutional limits.

The Atlantic. "The Normalization of Political Violence in America." March 2025. An analysis of how rhetoric, policy, and state-backed intimidation have moved political violence from the margins to the center of American public life.

NPR Investigations. "The Slow Dismantling of U.S. Election Oversight." April 2025. An in-depth examination of how state legislatures, partisan commissions, and weakened federal protections have systematically undermined election integrity.

Washington Post Special Report. "Democracy Under Siege: State Legislatures and the Erosion of Voting Rights." March 2025. A sweeping report on how Republican-controlled state governments are restricting access to voting, concentrating power, and dismantling independent election systems.

ABOUT THE AUTHOR

———— ✦ ————

Jim Vincent is a U.S. citizen, born and raised in the United States, where he lived for fifty years. He now resides in Australia, with children and grandchildren still living in the country he calls home. His writing reflects both an unbreakable connection to the American experiment—and a deep concern for its survival.

As an American living overseas, Vincent brings a perspective shaped by two advantages: distance from the tribal divisions that dominate U.S. politics, and the lived experience of another functioning democracy. From that vantage point, he sees with greater clarity what has been lost in the United States—and what remains possible.

He is the founder of *Jim Vincent US*, an independent publication focused on resisting authoritarianism and rebuilding democratic power. His work is trusted for its clarity, strategy, and moral purpose. He writes not for applause, but for action—believing that the republic must be reclaimed, not remembered.

He can be reached at https://jimvincentus.substack.com/

ALSO BY JIM VINCENT

American Renewal

Volume I of The American Renewal Trilogy

A manifesto for resistance, a blueprint for survival, and a plan to outlast authoritarian rule. Written to confront the second Trump presidency with truth, clarity, and strategic resolve.

American Restoration

Volume II of The American Renewal Trilogy

A comprehensive plan to rebuild the foundations of American democracy. Eighteen reforms necessary for rebuilding the foundations of democracy.

American Redemption *(forthcoming)*

Volume III of The American Renewal Trilogy

Eighteen legislative reforms to fulfill the constitutional promises—justice, peace, defense, prosperity, liberty, and unity—and build a republic that serves all its people.

Essays on Tyranny

A collection of essays on the collapse of American political norms between 2000 and 2024, and the cultural, moral, and institutional choices that made authoritarianism possible.

The Quiet Habit of Giving

A book about love, loss, and repair. Based on the six emotional needs that sustain long relationships—Admiration, Belonging, Control, Freedom, Security, and Validation—and what happens when they are missing.

For more, visit jimvincentus.substack.com.

www.ingramcontent.com/pod-product-compliance
Lightning Source LLC
Chambersburg PA
CBHW061212070526
44583CB00025B/3220